D0380586

The Truth About Reference Librarians

Other Books by Will Manley and Richard Lee

For Library Directors Only/For Library Trustees Only (McFarland, 1993)
The Manley Art of Librarianship (McFarland, 1993)
Uncensored Thoughts (McFarland, 1994)
The Truth About Catalogers (McFarland, 1995)

Other Books by Will Manley

Snowballs in the Bookdrop (1982)
Unintellectual Freedoms (McFarland, 1991)
Unprofessional Behavior (McFarland, 1992;
illustrations by Gary Handman)
Unsolicited Advice (McFarland, 1992;
illustrations by Gary Handman)

Other Books by Richard Lee

*You Can Tell Your Kid Will Grow Up
to Be a Librarian When...* (McFarland, 1992)

The Truth About Reference Librarians

by WILL MANLEY

Illustrations by
RICHARD LEE

with a foreword by
GERTRUDE MUSTARD STRONG

McFarland & Company, Inc., Publishers
Jefferson, North Carolina, and London

British Library Cataloguing-in-Publication data are available

Library of Congress Cataloguing-in-Publication Data

Manley, Will, 1949–
　　The truth about reference librarians / by Will Manley ; illus-
trations by Richard Lee; with a foreword by Gertrude Mustard
Strong.
　　　　p.　cm.
　　Includes index.
　　ISBN 0-7864-0220-2 (sewn softcover : 55# alk. paper) ∞
　　1. Reference services (Libraries)—United States—Humor.
I. Title.
Z711.M356　1996
025.52—dc20　　　　　　　　　　　　　　　　　　　96-1461
　　　　　　　　　　　　　　　　　　　　　　　　　　CIP

Manufactured in the United States of America

McFarland & Company, Inc., Publishers
　Box 611, Jefferson, North Carolina 28640

Acknowledgments

A book like this that attempts to tackle all aspects of contemporary reference librarianship first and foremost requires years of practical experience and field research, but it also benefits immensely from the collaborative help of dedicated reference colleagues. It's been my good fortune to pick the brains of some of the most interesting reference librarians of my (or any other) generation.

For starters, I called on my good friend Virgil Barkhole, long time reference librarian at the Gravel Point (TX) Public Library. From his prison cell in Waco, Virgil was charitable enough to share with me the details of his well publicized mental breakdown at the Gravel Point Public Library reference desk, the one in which he shot a library patron who asked for "a book with a yellow cover that was published in the 1970's." Thanks, Virgil!

Cynthia F. Bottomley, staff reference librarian for the Eggington Institute of Information, offered me invaluable information about her secret life as an infomaniac. Depressing as it was to hear her discuss her obsessive inability to bring a reference search to closure (before seeking therapy, she would sneak back into the library after closing to continue her research for hours), she did impart important insights into the "reference librarians who research too much" syndrome. Thanks, Cynthia!

The chapter on library patrons simply could not have been done without help from Maxwell A. Tuttle. I caught up with Tuttle at the Illinois State Mental Hospital in Galesburg, Illinois, where Tuttle has been residing for the past twenty years. You librarians, who like me are getting a "little long in the tooth," will remember Tuttle as the library patron serial killer who plied his trade in the early 1970's (both as a serial killer and reference librarian) at the Gadston (IL) Public Library. While Tuttle's insights into patron behavior were interesting, I couldn't help but wonder why Virgil Barkhole (who wounded one patron with a pistol) was in a maximum security prison in Texas while Tuttle (who viciously killed 17 patrons with a card catalog rod) would be enjoying life in a nuthouse in Illinois. Oh well, that's American justice for you. Thanks, Maxwell!

Finally, it would be remiss of me not to mention the assistance I received from Harriet Belfry, the notorious polygamist who had the exact opposite problem of Maxwell Tuttle. Harriet was so attracted to her patrons that she couldn't help marrying them. This famous reference librarian who loved too much was actually wedded to five library patrons at the same time! Thanks Harriet!

In view of the participation of these reference librarians, I would like to point out that any errors of misinformation in this book should be attributed solely to them and not to me.

A Note About
the Illustrator

Richard Lee is the director of the Summerlin Branch Library in Las Vegas, Nevada. He has had numerous cartoons published in magazines ranging from that late and censorious rag *The Wilson Library Bulletin* to the very popular magazine *Biker World*. In addition to illustrating Will Manley's monthly column, Richard has his own regular feature in *American Libraries*. It is called "What Bugs Me!"

In professional library circles, Richard is especially known for his innovative outreach work. One of his groundbreaking outreach projects was the work he did from 1983 to 1995 going to Las Vegas strip joints to try to personally persuade the table dancers to give up their lucrative lives of sin and go to library school in pursuit of an M.L.S. It was a tough job, but Richard was the perfect person to handle it.

A Note About the Author

In his past lives Will Manley has been a cave painter in southern France, a snake charmer in the court of Ramses II, a water boy in the 540 B.C. Olympics, a spear carrier in the Roman Imperial Army, an alchemist in medieval Paris, the royal astrologer for Prince Henry the Navigator, and a snake oil salesman in the Mississippi River valley during the Civil War.

In his present life Manley has been a librarian for the last twenty-five years. His professional objective is to write a bestselling book about library science. So far he has been unsuccessful. None of his eight previous books has grabbed the imagination of the masses of American people and none have been translated into foreign languages. He has not appeared on the *Today Show*, the *Tonight Show*, or the *Late Show*, although he did do a forty-five second stint on the *C.B.S. Morning Show* with Diane Sawyer which no one apparently saw but his mother and father. He does have hope that if this book does not make the *New York Times* bestseller list it will at least be picked up by Fox as an animated television series. Manley's main leisure time activity is searching through *AACR2* for the meaning of life, and his biggest fantasy is that some day one of his three sons will say, "Yeah, Dad, you're right."

Table of Contents

Foreword

I knew Will Manley when he first broke into the library profession as a raw reference librarian right out of library school. In fact I was his supervisor. Like most new recipients of the M.L.S. degree, Manley thought he knew it all. He was so full of himself and his 1960's spirit of idealism that it made the rest of us on staff quite sick. All his talk about the public library being the "University of the People" was just so much poppycock to us. Most of us on staff had been battling it out in the reference trenches before Manley had even learned to tie his left shoe. We knew the public for what it really was—a motley collection of ungrateful ignoramuses. It's hard to believe now but Manley was so idealistic that he even played around with the idea of doing a special adult storytime in the library parking lot for street people! That foolishness lasted about a week when one of Manley's favorite parking lot panhandlers pulled a gun on him and took his wallet.

After that unpleasantness Manley never seemed to be the same. He developed a less serious outlook on life. Saving the world no longer seemed to be on his agenda. Now all he wanted to do was have fun. Giving a hot foot in the staff room to Bertha "Big Mama" Babbey, who had been on her feet for four hours, was the kind of practical joke Manley became notorious for. Things went a little too far, however, when Manley spiked the board room coffee pot on the day that the library board was supposed to begin budget negotiations with the City Council.

Of course, we couldn't have that sort of thing, and so I had to discipline Will by banishing him to the cataloging room for a six month exile. This practically killed him. He called the cataloging room the "vegetable garden" and after only four days in that environment he claimed that he was beginning to breathe through his skin and was even starting to photosynthesize in bright sunlight. After only three weeks I had to pull him out of there before the regular catalogers killed him or he killed them.

In retrospect, all I can say is that 25 years ago, I never expected that

Manley would still be alive in 1995 let alone still be practicing as a librarian. I would have bet all the incense at the Vatican that he would have smarted off one time too many to a library patron and found himself sleeping with the fishes in the Little Calumet River.

There's absolutely no way he'll last another 25 years.

September 24, 1995
Gertrude Mustard Strong

(Publisher's Note: It looks like once again Will Manley gets the last laugh. Three days after writing this foreword, Miss Strong died in her office of a massive stroke. Donations should be sent to the Burned Out Reference Librarians International Relief Fund.)

Preface

"A WORD OF WARNING"

We've all tuned in to the local news only to see the broadcast start with a warning: "Those viewers who are offended by blood, gore, and dead bodies should turn off their television sets for the next two minutes." The effect of such a message of course is to make you stop whatever it is you are doing, walk over to the television set to get a better view of it, and turn up the volume. You don't want to miss a single image.

It is with that result in mind that I offer the following warning: Those readers who think that all reference librarians do all day is lead a quiet life of reading reference books and telling people how to get to the bathroom should shut this book and go do some needlepoint because the contents that lie within tell the real grim truth about life on the reference battlefield. Here you will read about psychotic patrons and homicidal reference librarians. This story is not always a pretty one, but it is true and it needs to be told.

Chapter 1

HOW DID REFERENCE SERVICES GET STARTED?

Origins of Reference Services

In the beginning was the word. Most historians agree that the first written records appeared in ancient Sumeria in 3500 B.C. The Sumerians scratched signs onto tablets of damp clay with a pointed stick that was called a stylus. The tablets were then left in the sun to bake. What resulted was a very durable and very stackable written record. At first hundreds of these records were produced and then thousands and then millions. The stacks of clay tablets got bigger and bigger and as they got bigger and bigger it became harder and harder to keep track of them. Obviously something had to be done to put them in order. That's when God sent to earth from a faraway galaxy a species of creature called the cataloger. In general these catalogers adapted well to earth conditions, but let's face it they've always been a little different from the rest of us. That's why the average ancient Sumerian library patron had as much trouble as the average modern American library patron in using the catalogs and indices created by catalogers. That's the reason reference librarians were hired—to help the public decipher the earliest clay tablet catalogs.

WHAT WERE THE FIRST
REFERENCE LIBRARIANS LIKE?

Ancient Sumeria was a dynamic, creative civilization that represented a revolutionary breakthrough for humankind. Before Sumeria tribes of humans roamed the earth hunting game and gathering seeds and berries. Oh there was the occasional town or village, but these were of a transitory nature. It wasn't until Sumeria that men and women gathered together on a permanent basis to form a true civilization complete with taxes, armies, and lawyers, the three hallmarks of a truly civilized society. The great thing about Sumeria was that for the first time since the creation of the world, young people no longer were limited to being either hunters or gatherers. Now their futures were unlimited. They could be almost anything—irrigation engineers, mathematicians, businessmen, architects, even metalworkers. That left the small minority of young people who went to college and majored in the humanities and had no technical or practical abilities other than the fact that they were great with people! So these "people persons" became the first reference librarians.

WHEN DID REFERENCE
SERVICES FIRST DEVELOP?

Most historians agree that full scale library reference service first appeared in the ancient Sumerian city of Uruk at the turn of the third millennium B.C. Not only have archeologists unearthed a series of what appear to be monthly reference statistical reports from that time period, but they have also discovered a clay tablet from that period that attacks catalogers for their continued use of "idiotic" subject headings. This clay tablet is naturally thought to be the work of a reference librarian. What is interesting about this tablet is that it represents the first shot fired in the 5,000 year old war that has been fought between catalogers and reference librarians. It's a war that can get downright nasty. Reference librarians love to refer to catalogers as "socially dysfunctional nitpickers" and catalogers love to catalog reference librarians under the subject heading "Imprecise, Impractical, and Illogical."

WHAT WAS THE FIRST REFERENCE
QUESTION EVER ASKED?

The first reference question asked is a subject of great speculation. For years librarians clung to a legend that was started in Victorian England by the great reference librarian of the British Museum, Gertrude Mustard Strong, who is often referred to as the Mother of Modern Reference. She claimed that the first reference question came from an inventor who needed to know how to file a patent application. It seems that he had just perfected a revolutionary invention called the wheel. Because the historical evidence for this claim is very scarce, most modern historians discount it as a self-serving myth. Archeologist Helmut Flapmeyer has a revisionist theory. After examining the remnants of the reference desk from the Royal Library of Uruk, he came to the conclusion that the first reference question was "Where's the bathroom?" What evidence does he have for this conclusion? He found a handmade bathroom directional sign on top of the reference desk. Using a highly sophisticated carbon dating process, Flapmeyer determined that this crudely made sign was just slightly younger than the desk itself. Obviously the first reference librarian got tired of pointing the way to the bathroom.

WHAT WAS THE FIRST
REFERENCE BOOK?

Up until about 2300 B.C. the concept of a specialized reference resource book had not been developed. In Sumeria there were clay tablets and in ancient Egypt there were papyrus scrolls, and in the earliest libraries these materials were arranged by order of accession number. There was no separate "ready reference" collection for the convenience of the reference staff. However, after years and years of answering the same question over and over again about the phases of the moon, the changing of the seasons, the long term weather outlook and the proper time to plant their crops, the reference librarians of the Edfu Community Library began to gather this information into a single scroll which they kept in the reference desk at all times. They called it *The Egyptian Farmer's Almanac*. Eventually, this handy little scroll earned a reputation for uncanny meteorological accuracy. Of course, Egyptian weather is not exactly a box of chocolates. You always know what you are getting—11 months of hot, dry weather followed by a month of flooding. Even today many people swear by *The Farmer's Almanac*. The meteorological predictions may not be as accurate, but the astrological charts are second to none.

WHO WAS THE FIRST PROBLEM PATRON?

In the ancient world reference services reached their peak during the flowering of classical Greece. This was a time of great intellectual ferment. Sophocles and Aeschylus were writing their tragedies, Thales was doing scientific experimentation, Aristophanes was composing poetry, and Socrates was asking questions. To be honest, Socrates was driving reference librarians nuts. He couldn't ask the normal questions that everyone else asked. He never needed anything quick and easy like a stock quotation or a demographic statistic. No, he wanted to know the answer to questions like "What is the meaning of life?" and "What is reality?" He became such a problem, that at the 106th annual Greek Library Association Conference, the RLRT (Reference Librarians Round Table) held an open forum on the topic "What Should Reference Librarians Do About Socrates?" Mysteriously the minutes to that meeting have never been found, and even more mysteriously three days later Socrates was found dead of hemlock poisoning.

WHEN AND WHERE DID READERS' ADVISORY SERVICES ORIGINATE?

It's quite clear that readers' advisory services started in Merry Old Elizabethan England. From 1592 to 1616 a certain playwright named Will Shakespeare drove the librarians at the East Bank Branch of the London Public Library quite nuts. True, Shakespeare was a gifted wordsmith with a genius for creating memorable passages of dialogue, but when it came to creating plots and stories for his Globe Theater scripts, he was not the most original thinker. If you were kind you'd call Shakespeare a great adapter, but if you were unkind you'd call him a plagiarist. That's right! Shakespeare stole all his stories from other writers. He ripped off *Hamlet*, for instance, from a popular play entitled *Ur-Hamlet* written by Thomas Kyd. Who was Shakespeare's literary accomplice in crime? It was a lowly reference librarian named Charles Uruquart who attended to all of Shakespeare's library needs. Apparently Shakespeare would come into the library and say, "I'm interested in reading a murder story which involves kings, queens, and ghosts. What do you recommend?" That's how readers' advisory services got started.

WHEN AND WHERE DID THE REFERENCE INTERVIEW ORIGINATE?

Many people do not know that Dr. Sigmund Freud, the father of psychoanalysis, originally set out to be a reference librarian. In fact, after receiving his doctorate in library studies at the University of Vienna Graduate School of Library Science, young Sigmund was retained by the University to work in the reference department where he was encouraged to experiment with new techniques in communicating with patrons. Dr. Freud's doctoral dissertation was entitled "What Do Patrons Want?" and his breakthrough research showed conclusively that library patrons rarely articulate their real informational needs because of unconscious feelings of shame and repression. It was Freud's theory that the role of the reference librarian was to uncover the real needs of the patron by engaging in an openended process that he called "patron psychoanalysis." To help the patron relax, a couch was set up adjacent to the reference desk. While Freud's questioning process lives on today as the reference interview, the couch is no longer standard reference equipment. It seems too many patrons were falling asleep during Freud's long and laborious series of questions.

HOW AND WHEN DID TELEPHONE REFERENCE SERVICES ORIGINATE?

Yes, Alexander Graham Bell was the inventor of the telephone. Every second grader knows that. What most people do not know was that for the greater part of his scientific career, Bell was totally focused on studying, researching, and experimenting in the area of teaching the deaf to speak. Bell basically lived in his laboratory while working non-stop on a new and revolutionary theory of vocal physiology. He was so obsessed with his research that he absolutely hated to even take time to eat meals. He considered going to the library to look up information as a considerable waste of his precious time. "If only I could access the library collection without having to physically go there I could save hundreds of valuable hours," he said to himself one day. The rest of the story is that Bell diverted himself away from his physiological studies just long enough to invent the telephone, and of course reference services were never the same.

HOW AND WHERE DID INFORMATION AND REFERRAL SERVICES ORIGINATE?

Many librarians take pride in the fact that Mao Zedong, the founder of the People's Republic of China, was a librarian in his early years as a young urban professional. It has even been stated that the Chinese Revolution started in the library where Mao worked. The premise is that Mao's exposure to the literary works of Marx, Engels, and Lenin provided him with the intellectual framework that he needed to lead the Chinese people in a new direction. This is only partially true. Actually Mao's experience in the public library brought him into contact with the many downtrodden people who were in search of a better life. In a manifesto entitled, "The Librarian as Revolutionary" Mao argued that these people didn't need books as much as they needed information about and referral to health and human services agencies. Thus began the concept of Information and Referral services. You may wonder why Mao left the library profession. The answer is simple. He quickly found out that there were no health and human services agencies in China to refer patrons to. Setting out to do something about that, Mao left the library and formed the People's Liberation Army.

Chapter 2

PASSAGES: TEN STAGES IN THE LIFE OF A REFERENCE LIBRARIAN

All good reference librarians know that about twenty years ago library patrons were lined up and waiting for a hot bestseller entitled *Passages*. The premise of the book was that all people evolve through a series of very definable life changes. There's the identity crisis, the mid-life crisis, the aging crisis, and so on until you die. What most reference librarians didn't realize at the time that they were dispensing this book to all their eager readers is that they have their own special series of passages called the "reference life cycle."

PASSAGE #1: I WANT
TO HELP HUMANITY

A stage one reference librarian is an eager beaver. This is a person who wants to serve the cause of educating all of humanity. The premise is not only that humanity is educable but that once educated it will become kind, gentle, productive, and peaceful. These are the kind of sentences that flow from the mouths of stage one reference librarians:

"I envision the public library as the university of the people."

"It's the diversity of patrons that draws me to reference. I love the opportunity to serve the young and old, rich and poor, well educated and poorly educated."

"I believe in giving equal service to everyone. The lowest street person gets the same level of service as the Mayor."

Of course if the stage one reference librarian really implements that last sentiment, he or she will never make it to stage two. Her future will be in the unemployment line.

PASSAGE #2: I WANT
TO HELP A FEW WORTHY PEOPLE

It takes about three months for our wide eyed idealist to grudgingly admit that not all of humanity is worth saving. Three months of being exposed to a diverse array of flashers, perverts, panhandlers, harassers, bawling children, and condescending professors will take its toll on even the perkiest new library school graduate. Oh, there is still a wellspring of idealism in our fledging reference librarian, but it's a more manageable type of idealism. It involves sincerely helping the one or two really worthy patrons and learning to tolerate the hundreds of jerks.

PASSAGE #3: AT LEAST I'M GETTING PAID FOR THIS MADNESS

At about the six month point our reference librarian is pretty much drained of all idealism. Bursts of anger and bouts of despondency occur more frequently as moments of abuse and stupidity multiply. The job, however, still has one redeeming factor—it is still a job. That's right. While the average reference librarian may have entered the profession as a mighty quest, he or she now sees it simply as a source of income. The fact that they give you a bi-weekly paycheck makes it all worthwhile, especially when you consider some of the jobs that other people have to endure to eke out a living like disposing of nuclear wastes, removing asbestos insulation, and teaching third grade students. But then again nuclear waste disposers, asbestos removers, and third grade teachers do not have to work nights and weekends.

PASSAGE #4: A REAFFIRMATION OF FAITH IN THE INHERENT VIRTUE OF REFERENCE WORK

The one year anniversary is a milestone date for the average reference librarian. It's a time for him or her to look back and evaluate the decision to get into the library profession. Yes, the satisfactions have been few, the frustrations have been many, and the compensation has been only slightly higher than what non-union fork lift operators make, but still the concept of helping the public with their informational needs will certainly count significantly with God at the final day of reckoning. Lacking the traditional forms of validation (like money and respect), our reference librarian falls back on a self-righteous sense of virtue to justify the mistake of actually going into debt to go to library school in order to torture oneself for life at the reference desk.

PASSAGE #5: REALITY REASSERTS ITSELF

Not to sound cynical, but the fact is that as C.S. Lewis states in his classic book, *The Screwtape Letters*, many religious conversions do not last very long. The problem with dedicating yourself to the concept of an afterlife is that you still have this life to deal with. Virtue does not pay the bills, and goodness does not necessarily give you the respect you crave from society. In a relatively short time, therefore, the ardent young reference librarian can be feeling quite miserable again. To make matters worse, in his renewed quest to help humanity our fervent librarian makes the mistake of pulling out his wallet to give the panhandler who works the library parking lot a dollar. Naturally the panhandler pulls out a gun and grabs the librarian's wallet. The irony of course is that of all the people to rob, a librarian is one of the least likely to be carrying around any serious cash. The damage done, therefore, is more emotional than financial.

PASSAGE #6: MAYBE I OUGHT TO TRANSFER TO CATALOGING

If you're a reference librarian it is quite easy to identify the exact time when you were first stricken with an unadulterated and irreversible sense of disillusionment. It was the moment you woke up and for the first time in your life you saw cataloging as a noble calling. What a contrast that perspective is to the one you had in library school when you were forced to suffer the indignity of taking Cataloging 101 from a misanthropic professor. Since then you have stereotyped all catalogers as socially dysfunctional nitpickers who are unable to relate well to people and other living things. Now, however, you see cataloging as your escape hatch, a way to make use of your library degree without having to deal with stupid patrons. Unfortunately for our hero a transfer to cataloging is out of the question for one very simple reason. There are no openings. Once hired, catalogers never leave. Sometimes they die but even then it takes a while to figure out that they're dead.

PASSAGE #7: IT'S TIME TO START TAKING AN INTEREST IN THE AMERICAN LIBRARY ASSOCIATION

The American Library Association is a very big three ring circus with a wonderful diversity of sideshows. The organization is valuable because it serves many different purposes for many different types of librarians. One of its most important functions is to provide a life raft to librarians who are in a mid career crisis, which is precisely the situation our reference librarian is floundering around in. Disillusioned by reference and unable to get into cataloging, our heroine sees organizational involvement as a road to personal development and professional respect. The problem, however, is that is precisely what the other 56,000 members of A.L.A. are striving to find. As a consequence, A.L.A. is a dog-eat-dog world that only exacerbates stress and alienation.

PASSAGE #8: DON'T CHANGE JOBS; CHANGE TITLES

There was one productive aspect to our hero's foray into A.L.A. politics. She became exposed to the brave new world of technological jargon. From attending many A.L.A. programs and committee meetings she learned that those professions which traffic in the electronic warehousing and delivery of information and research data will grow and prosper in our emerging world of the information superhighway. In this new phase of her professional life, therefore, our reference librarian fancies herself as an information scientist, a title which sounds so much more impressive than reference librarian. With renewed vigor our heroine dedicates herself to mastering the new electronic tools of the library trade, and within weeks she is able to conduct a highly sophisticated Boolean search in the twinkling of a diode. Our new information scientist is wired with a new enthusiasm for her job.

PASSAGE #9: THINK VIRTUAL

It turns out unfortunately that this vision of the reference librarian as a broker on the information superhighway is a bit premature. While there is certainly an explosion of information going on in such revolutionary fields as biomedical engineering, ergotic orbit studies, and frog communication, these don't seem to be the types of areas that interest most library patrons. So while the average reference librarian has instant electronic access to a growing base of information in a wide diversity of sophisticated fields, the average library patron still seems to have stone age level requests. Once our reference librarian comes to this inevitable conclusion, it is only a matter of a few short months that the trendy notion of the "virtual library" (which solely serves the electronic elite plugged in at home and not the Neanderthals who actually go to the library) will look tantalizingly attractive. Infatuation with this vision will die as soon as the reference librarian realizes that without real patrons she has no job. This is the unavoidable truth about reference librarianship. Reference librarians exist to help stupid patrons. It's a symbiotic relationship. Without stupid patrons there would be no need for reference librarians.

PASSAGE #10: I'M A LIFER
AND PROUD OF IT!

Once the reference librarian accepts the fact that she is inextricably linked to her patrons, a fact that cannot be altered by technology, she has a decision to make to get out of the profession for good or become a lifer. There is a certain serenity to be gained from accepting the inevitable. The reference librarian can now proceed with her life with a minimum of confusion and anxiety. She knows her destiny is not to radiate with the glittering vision of the information scientist but to work obscurely and diligently in the difficult process of building bridges for real people to cross from the fading world of books and the advancing universe of electronics. There is little fanfare in this modest but important work, and the satisfactions are few, but every now and then when you least expect it someone says "thank you."

Chapter 3

HATS

Generally when we think of librarians, we don't think of the best dressed profession under the sun. There are a couple of reasons for this. One, there's the matter of money. It takes a lot of money to develop a *G.Q.* or *Vogue* kind of image, money that the average reference librarian would rather spend on something more basic like food, shelter, and more importantly books. And then there's the little matter of comfort. Reference librarians are always on their feet running between the stacks, the catalog, and the desk. A comfortable look is not always a stylish look. But when it comes to hats, reference librarians are second to none. That's because they wear so many of them. One minute they're a doctor, next minute a lawyer, and the next an auto mechanic. In fact a few simple mathematical calculations reveal that if reference librarians were paid at market rates for all the roles they play, they would have salaries well over $200,000.

MEDICAL DOCTOR

Why is it that so many people bring their very personal medical problems to the reference desk? Is it because reference librarians are cheaper, more knowledgeable, or have a better bedside manner than the average heart specialist or oncologist? Actually the truth probably lies in the fact that most reference librarians are more dedicated in their search for truth. There's something quite reassuring to a patron about a professional who is willing to spend time actually providing a wealth of background information about his or her condition. That's much more comforting than the usual take two aspirin and drink plenty of fluids advice that the average doctor gets paid $78 for. If, however, we librarians really do want to be taken seriously as health care providers, we really need to stop putting the pregnancy books on the bottom shelf. That's not at all a funny situation for the woman who is eight months pregnant and is carrying twins.

LAWYER

The fact that reference librarians get plenty of legal questions is not surprising. Lawyers are simply too expensive for the average citizen to consult for every little dog bite, fist fight, or marital spat. Plus there's a great tradition in our country to act as your own attorney. Equal protection under the law irrespective of socioeconomic status is one of the great philosophical pillars upon which our justice system is based. Unfortunately libraries, rather than law firms, are where most common people turn to get their knowledge of federal, state, and local statutes. What are you going to do when your landlord boots you out of your apartment just because you're a couple of months in arrears? Are you going to call a lawyer or a reference librarian? In nine cases out of ten you're going to go to the reference librarian for help. And guess what? Not only will you pay a lot less, you'll also probably get better service.

HOME HANDYMAN

I am absolutely convinced that the man who started Home Depot was at one point in his career a reference librarian. As a reference librarian he would have learned that most middle class Americans are either too proud or too cheap to call in a pro to replace a garbage disposal, fix a wallpaper seam, re-wire a faulty socket, or caulk a bathtub. Next to the public library, Home Depot has become America's foremost gathering place for home handymen. It's a place where you can not only buy an automatic garage door opener but also attend a free class on how to install it. The staff there are all very friendly, very helpful, and very knowledgeable. Unfortunately for reference librarians there are many neighborhoods and entire communities that are not served by a Home Depot. That leaves the public library reference desk as the place to go for do it yourself help, and certainly there are many good books on the subject, but that's never enough. Most patrons want more. They want the warm, personal advice of a reference librarian, which is scary because if the average reference librarian had any technical skills at all he or she would never have become a reference librarian in the first place!

WALL STREET WIZARD

Probably the greatest continuing myth about America is that this is a country where anyone can strike it rich. Unfortunately there is just enough truth in that myth to make it dangerous. Ordinary people look at idiots like Rush Limbaugh, Howard Stern, Roseanne, Tom Arnold, and Kato Kaelin and they firmly believe that with the right timing and the right idea they too can become rich and famous. Unfortunately they have the mistaken notion that wealth results more from luck than work. So while these Donald Trump wannabees are ambitious to become rich their ambition does not carry with it much of a work ethic. Their real role model is Hillary Clinton who parlayed $1,000 into well over $100,000 in a few short months in the futures market. Yes, like Hillary, they see securities and commodities as their tickets to the good life, and who better to consult for hot stock market tips than their friendly neighborhood reference librarian. Just how stupid are these people? If we had inside information do they really think we'd a) share it with them or b) be working the reference desk?

CAR MECHANIC

Americans love to drive cars and cars love to break down. We've all had the experience of having a bad carburetor and making the mistake of taking it to a garage. The bill is always maddening—$17 for parts and $177 for labor. Owning a car wouldn't be half bad if we could just eliminate those $177 bills for labor. That's why public libraries put so much money into their automotive repair collections. The public demands it. People would rather spend the $177 on something far more productive, like state lottery tickets. The problem is, however, that most auto repair manuals are incomprehensible. It's easier to read a line of Egyptian hieroglyphics than an auto repair schematic. Fortunately the average reference librarian is fairly knowledgeable in this area. Why? Because we of all people can least afford to have our cars fixed professionally. So out of necessity we have learned that auto mechanics make the best spouses. That's right. A recent research study reveals that more reference librarians marry car mechanics than any other type of person. And when a particularly difficult auto repair question gets asked all we have to do is, you guessed it, call our spouse.

TAX ACCOUNTANT

About ten years ago some overly patriotic reference librarian made a suggestion to the Internal Revenue Service that he said would save them millions of dollars. Why not, he advised, use libraries as tax form distribution centers. Unfortunately not only did the I.R.S. jump on this suggestion like a dog on a popsicle, but so did many library directors. They felt that by distributing tax forms, their libraries would attract many new users. How right they were. From April 1 to April 15 a whole hive of tax evaders, procrastinators, and freeloaders swarmed upon us with the intensity of angry yellow jackets. As a result the average American library resembled a cross between an I.R.S. office and an H. and R. Block franchise. And what about the average reference librarian? He or she became the object of abuse, threats, and demands. Turning the library into a subdivision of the Internal Revenue Service has been the biggest public relations blunder for libraries since the day that Marian the Librarian raised her right index finger to her lips and hissed "shhh."

EMPLOYMENT SPECIALIST

Walk into any public library during the middle of the day when all the students are in school and whom do you find? There are basically three types of people: a) retirees, b) mothers of pre-school children, and c) the unemployed. If you've lost your job and you're in the habit of going somewhere everyday where do you go? The library is the only place where if you're in shirt and shoes and you're not bothering anyone, no one will bother you. Plus the library has the added advantage of having the best collection of newspaper classified ads in town. Not only that but the reference librarian is there to assess your occupational skills and advise you as to your career path. Of course that can be very difficult if you have no computer skills, no technical ability, no job experience, and are not a "people person."

Chapter 4

A FIELD GUIDE TO REFERENCE PESTS AND OTHER LIBRARY INSECTS

The library is the natural habitat for a wide diversity of pests. Because of the central location of the reference desk in most libraries, it is typically the responsibility of the reference staff to deal with those species of unpleasant patrons who make life difficult for the rest of us. Keeping these pests under control, however, is no easy task. Zookeepers, prison wardens, and nut house psychiatrists have an easier time of it than reference librarians. That's because the reference librarian is committed to respect a little inconvenience of democracy called the First Amendment. Yes, the First Amendment insures us access to a whole universe of books and information, but it also means that everyone from the neighborhood drug dealer to the flasher who lives under the Main Street Bridge has free and open access to our libraries. What follows is a field guide to some of the more annoying species of library pests.

DORKUS COMPLETIS

This smallish hard shelled bug is commonly known as a geek or a dweeb. This is the species of library patron that wants some minute factoid of information that you know doesn't exist because he himself can't find it. What you're not completely sure of is this pest's intentions. Does he really need to find out where he can buy an H.O. scale model of Mount Rushmore or is he just trying to drive you crazy? Actually his intentions are probably sincere because the *Dorkus completis* is just the kind of geek who plays with model trains well into adulthood.

How to eradicate: This bug is basically wimpy. Don't waste any time on him. Step on him quickly and he will crack. The words, "That information is not available in this library!" will usually send him scurrying to some other library.

JERKUS DISGUSTIS

This quick moving, winged pest is better known as the freckle-bellied flasher. He rarely lights in one place in the library but seems to hover everywhere. Anyone wearing an oversized rain coat on a warm, sunny day is a good bet to be a *Jerkus disgustis*. This most unpleasant creature enjoys preying upon unsuspecting women of all ages. That's because most men would find him a loathsome bore. To women he is more of a loathsome boor especially when he exposes his private appendages in a most sudden and intimate fashion. Although he is physically harmless he can cause great psychological damage to his victims.

How to eradicate: Trap him back in the stacks with a police stake-out and throw him in jail. Then throw away the key.

PERVERTUS HORRIBILIS

Many people often confuse the *Jerkus disgustis* with the *Pervertus horribilis*. Actually these are two distinctly different pests. While the flasher is an annoyance that can cause psychological pain, the pervert's sting is much more serious. He can cause real mental and even more physical damage. Whereas the flasher openly attempts to display his privatemost parts to random passersby, the pervert surreptitiously attempts to peep at the privatemost parts of a few selected victims. He can often be found holding a hand mirror to aid this discovery process. The *Pervertus horribilis* is often confused with the *Populus commonus*. It's a common misconception that perverts are unshaven and unsavory street people. Actually many perverts are perfectly ordinary Republican church goers who hide behind a false veil of respectability.

How to eradicate: Approach the pervert straightforwardly and say, "Sir, we have been watching you and you are creating the distinct impression that the only reason you came to the library today was to look up women's dresses." In most cases the pervert will quickly flee and never come back.

POPULUS COMMONUS

This pest is a mere annoyance, a common fact of life that inhabits all types and sizes of libraries. It is also known by the names bum, vagrant, hobo, and street person. This species is the library patron equivalent of the common house fly. Groups of these pests can be seen congregating at the front door five minutes before opening like flies clinging to a screened kitchen window. Although the *Populus commonus* often emits a rather unpleasant pungent odor, he is usually a harmless individual who wants to be left alone to warm up, read the newspaper, and sleep. If provoked with threats or admonitions, this pest can be transformed into a loud and potentially dangerous creature. He is best left alone.

How to eradicate: This species is too numerous to eradicate. It can, however, be controlled with a little Lysol and a lot of empathy.

READERUS MURDERIS

Paint this pest—the murder mystery reader—with a ghoulish smile. There's nothing that makes this species of library patron happier than a well conceived homicide. Some sprinkles of arsenic in a dry martini, a well placed blow to the head with a tire iron, a sterling silver carving knife in the back, and an expertly wired car bomb—these are the nuances of crime that keep murder mystery fans coming back for more. Actually this pest's mosquito like thirst for literary blood can get a bit tiresome for the harried reference librarian. The constant buzzing in the ear—"Why did you only buy 59 copies of the latest P.D. James novel?" "Where is my name on the waiting list for the new Ed McBain thriller?"—can become murderous indeed.

How to eradicate: The next time a crime novel addict asks for the latest murder mystery, give the plot away.

GENEALOGUS JUNKIS

For sheer intensity there is no other library patron that rivals the amateur genealogist, a species that is often referred to by reference librarians as the "genie junkie." This pest feels that the library exists for one reason and one reason only—to help him trace his family tree. For this patron no genealogical resource is too obscure or too expensive for the library to acquire. You say you can't afford to buy the 1790 microfilmed census rolls? Just cancel your subscriptions to *Time*, *Newsweek*, and *Money* magazines. You don't think you can fit one more microfilm reader in your audiovisual room? Just get rid of some of your bulky CD-ROM reader-printers.

How to eradicate: The next time a genie junkie calls and requests your assistance in tracing his family tree, just call him back in five minutes and say, "Eureka! We've traced your family history back 5,000 years to a woman in the Middle East named Eve!"

PUPILUS GIFTIS

This pest is better known as the "gifted student." By strict definition one or two percent of our elementary school population is intellectually gifted. Unfortunately, 100% of all parents think that their children are in this one to two percent genius category. Think hard. When is the last time you heard a parent say, "My child is average." The fact of the matter is that in an effort to appease parents, weak kneed educators have promulgated the myth that all children are in their own way gifted. The irony of course is that standardized testing scores reveal that elementary students have recently reached new depths of stupidity. The problem for reference librarians is that the pushy parents of these "gifted" children think that the books in the children's library are too infantile to challenge their child's intellect and so they request adult books that their little geniuses can understand. This request is, of course self contradictory.

How to eradicate: The next time the mother of a "gifted" child requests a book for that child, give her a copy of Jean-Paul Sartre's *Being and Nothingness* and say that it has become all the rage in the ten year old gifted set.

STUDENTUS MORONIS

The term moronic student is getting to be somewhat redundant isn't it? What are they teaching students these days in high school and college? Our nation would appear to be in grave danger. Not only do today's students have trouble speaking in simple declarative statements with subject/verb agreement, but many of them cannot even tell you why we celebrate the 4th of July. The male version of the species is characterized by baseball hats worn backwards and pants worn low and baggy. The females often sports incongruous clothing combinations such as mini-skirts with combat boots. Both genders are marked by multiple earrings and tattoos. Serving this brain dead pest is a real challenge. How do you remain tactful and polite when some baggy panted junior college student shuffles up to you and says, "Dude, I need a copy of the newspaper from the day that Jesus Christ was born."

How to eradicate: The next time a clueless student comes up to you five minutes before closing and demands five sources for a research paper on suicide, give him Dr. Kevorkian's latest "how-to" manual.

PARENTUS IRRESPONSIBILIS

This species of pest—the irresponsible parent—can be detected less by its own physical appearance and more by the sounds emanating from its offspring. If you are in the adult reference area and you hear a child crying, screaming, whining, chortling, gurgling, shrieking, or howling, you can bet that there is a *Parentus irresponsibilis* nearby. Look for a younger parent, someone who fits in the Generation X mold. The vacant, moronic glaze on the face is a dead giveaway. Most of these pests are brain dead and/or hearing impaired from listening to too much heavy metal. That is why their children's blatant public misbehavior does not bother them. Screaming is not a cacophonous distraction for them; it is part of the wallpaper of their lives.

How to eradicate: Eradication of this pest is very difficult mainly because nothing seems to offend this species of slacker. Everything is "cool" to them. Putting duct tape on the child's mouth, however, will at least stop the noise.

EDUCATUS PERKIS

The perky teacher is the bumble-bee of library pests. She's always buzz, buzz, buzzing around the library demanding that you get this book for her on inter-library loan, that you put these books on reserve for her class, that you give her unlimited check-out periods, that you forgive the fines of her students, and that you remove all restrictions for her on the number of books that she can have checked out at any given time. Why does she want all these special privileges? It's because she has dedicated her life to educating young people and the least you can do is help her in this holy quest. This all sounds very reasonable until you consider there are literally hundreds of teachers in any given community. One bumble-bee is an annoyance, a whole hive of them is a health hazard.

How to eradicate: Never, ever give special privileges to any teacher because you'll end up giving the same privileges to all of them and pretty soon your entire library collection will be dispersed in classrooms all over town.

PROFESSORUS ABSENTMINDEDNIS

The absent-minded professor has traditionally been regarded as an endearing old eccentric. Remember how Fred McMurray played the role in the old "Flubber" movies? Yes, he was a scientific genius, but let's not forget how inept he was at mastering the more mundane aspects of human existence, like remembering to take the trash out to the front curb every Wednesday morning. It's that lack of attention to everyday details that puts the absent-minded professor high up on the pest list for reference librarians. It is most annoying, for instance, when the professor assigns a research paper on esoteric subjects without taking the time to determine whether or not the library has any information in these areas (which of course it never does). Who do the hordes of frustrated students take their anger out on? You guessed it—the hapless reference librarian.

How to eradicate: Unfortunately the absent-minded professor is a privileged pest who cannot be eradicated because of something called tenure. They will therefore continue to populate libraries as long as the world exists.

DWEEBUS CYBERIS

The cybernetic dweeb is also known by the names "hacker," "geek," and "nerd." This pest wants all his information to come from on-line sources. He nests for hours in the reference room and hogs one whole computer for hours at a time. He has also been known to print out over 300 sheets of hard copy off the library's printer, which he of course regards as his own private tool. It's ironic that a person so electronically oriented likes paper so much! This person gets very abusive with reference librarians who first go to book sources to answer his informational questions. "Don't waste my time with obsolete books!" seems to be his mating call.

How to eradicate: This pest disappears during electrical storms that knock out the power to the library and cause the computer system to crash. The best way to eradicate him, herefore, is to learn some good violent rain dances.

PESTUS HARASSIS

Of all the pests that reference librarians have to deal with the harasser is the most troublesome on a day to day basis. These cretins come in all shapes, sizes, genders, and ages. They can be identified more by their obnoxious behavior than by their outward appearance. In a word the harasser treats the library staff like dirt. They torment reference librarians with threats, insults, and unreasonable demands. The man who leers at you and makes sexual remarks, the woman who demands that you give her immediate attention when the phones are ringing and patrons are lined up at the desk, the salesman who threatens to call the Mayor if you do not let him check out the local business directory, and the irate taxpayer who demands that you personally devote your day to his information search because he pays your salary are all common examples of the harassing patron.

How to eradicate: These harassers are unfortunately the library equivalent of cockroaches. They resist all attempts at extermination. As long as there are libraries there will be tormenting patrons.

Chapter 5

A FIELD GUIDE TO REFERENCE LIBRARIANS

Patrons are not the only inhabitants of libraries that can be classified and cataloged. Despite the stereotyped image that the general public has of librarians, we are not all repressed nerds who wear our hair in a bun and favor nineteenth century clothes. The truth is that there is a great deal of diversity among reference librarians. What follows is a field guide to that diversity.

THE FREUDIAN ANALYST

The reference interview is supposed to be a give and take between the patron and the librarian. What the reference librarian is attempting to do is determine the exact informational need of the patron. Often times a specific need is hidden in a general question. If, for example, a patron asks for books on dogs, you can bet that what he or she really wants is information about a specific type of dog. The trick for the reference librarian is to ferret this information out without seeming to be nosy or impolite. Unfortunately some reference librarians do not know when to stop. To them the reference interview is an encounter session. They feel that one more question will reveal the latent desires and hidden motives of the patron. They probably read too much Freud in college.

THE BOOKWORM

Let's be honest about it. Many of us got into the library profession because we flat out love books. Books are our passion, our obsession, our very reason for existence. We love their texture, their smell, and the way they fit so comfortably into our hands. Given the choice of living without food or books, we'd rather have the books. This is a problem for us when we work reference because we much prefer hunkering down at the service counter to peruse all the newly acquired books than helping give patrons access to them. In fact we're very possessive about our libraries' books. We don't enjoy sharing them with patrons who might not appreciate them as much as we do.

THE INFODWEEB

This is the reference librarian who is mesmerized by anything that comes across a cathode ray screen. There's something about a blinking computer cursor that gives this type of librarian a real adrenaline rush. The infodweeb's favorite activity is surfing the Internet. He or she just loves to sit at the computer terminal and explore every backroad and byway of the information superhighway. The problem with this is that the infodweeb, like his print counterpart the bookworm, becomes oblivious to the line of people at the desk waiting to be helped.

THE INFOMANIAC

The infomaniac is the reference librarian who researches too much. This person's affliction is an inability to bring a reference search to closure. He or she is obsessive about checking every possible reference source imaginable to answer even the simplest of patron requests. Suppose, for example, a patron simply wants to know how to spell the word, "serendipity." The infomaniac will not just look it up in any old desk dictionary at the reference counter, but will also validate the word's definitive spelling, by checking several unabridged dictionaries. When the infomaniac gets a really tough question like "How much does an eagle's nest weigh?" he or she will be of no use the rest of the day, but will spend literally hours researching the problem.

THE CLINICALLY DEPRESSED

This is the reference librarian who is on information overload. If ignorance produces bliss, it stands to reason that knowledge produces depression. This is an occupational hazard because reference librarians are exposed to literally mountains of information on a whole diversity of unpleasant subjects like pollution, crime, diseases, famines, natural disasters, war, and corruption just to name a few. This person can be identified by his or her total inability to smile or say anything positive about human existence, and the more information this person absorbs, the more he or she despairs. This is a librarian that you definitely do not want to send to Dr. Kevorkian for the annual wellness checkup.

THE INFO SNOB

This is the species of reference librarian who actually believes that academic degrees mean something. You can often hear this person say, "I did not go to college for four years and graduate school for two, just to show some post-print, functionally illiterate library patron where to find books on house cats." This is a person who wants to show off his or her knowledge of 13th century Gothic architecture and 20th century Boolean search strategies. Unfortunately the real world is rarely interested in those things. What does this librarian say to the patron who wants books on house cats? He says, "You don't really want a book on house cats you want a book on the symbolic role of cats in the Egyptian Book of the Dead from the second millennium B.C."

THE VALIDATION DEPRIVED

This librarian functions under the mistaken notion that library patrons will express their heartfelt thanks for the help they receive at the reference desk. When this gratitude is not forthcoming (which it rarely is), the librarian sinks into a depressing funk. There is a direct correlation between the amount of time a reference librarian spends on a question and the amount of appreciation that he or she expects to receive from the patron. The validation deprived librarian can become downright hostile when he spends four hours on a difficult research problem and calls the patron up with the right answer only to have the patron say, "Oh thanks, but I don't need the information anymore."

Chapter 6

HOW CAN YOU TELL IF YOU ARE SUFFERING FROM REFERENCE BURNOUT?

The great hazard of reference work is burnout. It's as inevitable as ring around the collar and yellow wax build-up. Burnout is what results from bending over backward eight hours everyday to please library patrons who are not particularly intelligent, appreciative, or even civil. The stress that results from burnout manifests itself in a wide diversity of warning signs. What follows are some of the more common warning signs that burnout has set in and that some kind of an intervention should be utilized to prevent the reference librarian from experiencing a psychotic episode with a library patron.

You might be suffering from reference burnout if you put plastic cockroaches on top of the reference desk to keep patrons away.

You might be suffering from reference burnout if you enjoy secretly affixing tattletapes to the backs of patrons whom you despise so that they will set off the security alarm when they exit the library.

You might be suffering from reference burnout if you are having a recurring dream about transferring to cataloging.

You might be suffering from reference burnout if you have been giving serious thought to joining an A.L.A. committee.

You might be suffering from reference burnout if a fat patron asks you for the latest diet book and you hand him a refrigerator lock.

You might be suffering from reference burnout if you decide to rearrange the current periodical collection by fragrance.

You might be suffering from reference burnout if you make funny faces at patrons as soon as they turn their backs to you.

You might be suffering from reference burnout if you begin all reference interviews by sneezing into the patron's face.

You might be suffering from reference burnout if you are in the habit of giving false directions whenever a patron asks where the restrooms are.

You might be suffering from reference burnout if you start hanging around the contagious diseases wing of the local hospital in hopes that you will have an opportunity to use some of your accumulated sick leave.

You might be suffering from reference burnout if you start using finger puppets to answer reference questions and you put the puppet on your middle finger.

You might be suffering from reference burnout if you hold yourself hostage in the corner of the reference workroom and threaten to pull the fire alarm if anyone comes near you.

You might be suffering from reference burnout if you like to trim your fingernails with the electric pencil sharpener.

You might be suffering from reference burnout if you refuse to believe the publication dates of old reference books and insist on carbon dating them for verification.

You might be suffering from reference burnout if you start introducing your coworkers to your good friend Melvil Dewey.

You might be suffering from reference burnout if you find yourself making obscene phone calls to fellow librarians.

You might be suffering from reference burnout if you begin every reference interview by saying, "Can you be helped?"

You might be suffering from reference burnout if you refuse to open any mail because you are convinced that the Unabomber is one of your disgruntled patrons.

You might be suffering from reference burnout if you begin breaking into the computer catalog late at night in order to catalog the new books the way you want them cataloged.

You might be suffering from reference burnout if you make sure that any items you send to mending will get proper attention.

You might be suffering from reference burnout if you instruct the fat guy who wants a diagnosis of an abdominal lump to go back to the reference office and take off all his clothes and wait for you to come back with a copy of *Gross Anatomy*.

You might be suffering from reference burnout if your supervisor begins chaining you to the desk to keep you from wandering in the stacks.

You might be suffering from reference burnout if you have decided to rearrange the reference collection by the size of each book.

You might be suffering from reference burnout if a patron asks for a "good mystery" and you hand her a copy of *AACR2*.

You might be suffering from reference burnout if you decide to put an anti-social bumper sticker on your car.

You might be suffering from reference burnout if you decide to "enhance" your library's signs with messages of your own.

You might be suffering from reference burnout if you can't restrain yourself from breaking into songs from Broadway musicals during the middle of reference interviews.

You might be suffering from reference burnout if you like to work the reference desk with a paper bag over your head.

You might be suffering from reference burnout if every time you answer the question "Where's the bathroom?" you record it on your daily tally sheet as a "Complex Research Question Answered Correctly."

You might be suffering from reference burnout if you go to the staff barbecue and announce to everyone there that according to the latest edition of *The International Encyclopedia of Food Values* there are 157 grams of fat in one hamburger and 237 grams of fat in each hot dog.

Chapter 7

RINGING PHONES AND RAGING PATRONS: HOW TO DEAL WITH REFERENCE BURNOUT

Don't you just love those books that have been coming out in the last ten years on how to cope with job stress. They have some really wonderful ideas, don't they? Yeah, right. Take a trip to Aruba. Buy a new wardrobe. Trade your stationwagon in for a European sportscar. Schedule an appointment every three days with a professional masseuse. Take a one year sabbatical and study the ancient Mayan ruins in Cancun. These are great ideas, but totally beyond the financial means of the average reference librarian. So what's the answer? How do impoverished library professionals deal with stress? The best way is to stay clear of patrons for a while. But how do you do this if you work reference? It's easy if you follow the unfriendly advice in this chapter's pages.

USE INAPPROPRIATE SIGNAGE

Probably the biggest unresolved and on-going issue in reference librarianship is what to call the "reference desk." To the average library patron the word "reference" is an ambiguous one that connotes the recommendations that you would normally use to secure a bank loan or get a job. Why a library would have a "reference" desk is therefore a source of wonderment to them. That's why many libraries call their reference desks by different names. The following are the most popular new terms:

Ask Here
Info to Go
Help Desk
Question Desk
Answer Desk

But if your goal is to reduce job stress by keeping patrons from asking stupid questions we suggest erecting the following sign over your desk: *Information Desk for People Who Are Too Stupid to Do Their Own Library Research!* You've got to admit that's a pretty accurate definition of reference service.

AVOID EYE CONTACT

To avoid patrons you must first and foremost avoid eye contact with them. The minute you make eye contact with a patron you are in trouble. Don't go looking for trouble. Eye contact signifies that you are a caring, sharing individual who is sincerely interested in helping some moron find information on the life cycle of a fruit fly. By making eye contact you are inviting a patron to ask you stupid questions. How can you avoid eye contact? Here are a few helpful hints: a) Wear very dark glasses and pretend that you are blind, b) Build a fortress of reference books around you and pretend that you are working really hard on a difficult reference question, or c) Grow your hair down over your eyes.

CREATE AN INAPPROPRIATE
REFERENCE DESK DECOR

Okay, you made your first mistake. Some persistent little pest was hovering around the desk, and in a moment of annoyance, you looked up at him. You made the mistake of making eye contact. He now knows that he is there. Your only hope now is that he will be repulsed by your offensive desk top decor. In creating an uninviting reference ambiance, start with the strategic placement of three or four rubber snakes. Great advancements have been made in the design and manufacture of artificial reptiles. If you really want to get gross use fake vomit. Plastic vomit today is virtually indistinguishable from the real thing. If that isn't sufficiently repulsive then I suggest you resort to placing a real dead rat right under the reference desk.

WEAR ANTI-SOCIAL BUTTONS

Many librarians like to wear inspirational message buttons like "Ban the bomb; don't ban books" or "Please disturb me. I am here to help you." What you want to do is wear a message button that will drive patrons away. Start with your staff name tag. Don't just wear a badge that says "Robert Jones." Wear a badge that says "Robert the Ripper Jones" or "Robert Killer Jones." Complement this with a button with an anti-social message. "What Part of No Don't You Understand" is a good one. Or how about this: "Genius at Work—Don't Bother Me with Stupid Questions."

COMMUNICATE WITH
NEGATIVE NON-VERBALS

This patron really needs something because he has penetrated your defensive barrier of fake insects, dead rodents, and obnoxious signs. Now is the time to fall back on your full repertoire of anti-social non-verbal behaviors. The following are very good at driving people away from you: a) Hack, sneeze, cough and then clear your throat, b) Cross your arms in the universal "stay away from me" position. c) Don't wash and never, ever use a deodorant, an anti-perspirant, or a cologne. d) Eat garlic and onion before going out to the desk. e) Frown at the patron. f) Wear vampire teeth. g) Pretend that you are experiencing a psychotic episode by breaking into tears for no apparent reason.

EMPLOY OFF-BEAT
COMMUNICATION TECHNIQUES

If your non-verbals do not repel the patron, you must now consider using one of the following communication behaviors: a) Fake laryngitis. b) Pretend that you are a mime. c) Speak in a heavy Hungarian accent. d) Use sign language. e) Communicate through a finger puppet on your middle finger. f) Pick up the phone and carry on a long involved phantom reference interview. g) Whistle "Stars and Stripes Forever." h) Fake deafness.

CULTIVATE ANNOYING PERSONAL HABITS

Why do marriages break down? Is it because couples have major differences over big issues like what house to buy or what community to live in? No, your average husband and wife can agree on the big things. It's the little things that drive people apart—the way you slurp your soup, the whistling sound that you make when you pronounce the letter "s," and the way you hum to yourself whenever you're feeling happy. These are the things that drive your partner to the divorce lawyer's office. The same thing holds true with patrons. Cultivate annoying habits and they'll learn to steer clear of you. Nail biting, hair twisting, nose picking, and head scratching are all effective turnoffs.

ALWAYS OPEN THE REFERENCE INTERVIEW WITH A QUESTION OF YOUR OWN

To drive patrons away it's always important to take control of the reference interview right from the start. Always respond to the patron's question with an immediate question of your own: *"Why do you want to know?"* If the patron says he is working on a homework assignment, say "I'm sorry it is the library's policy not to help students with homework." If the patron says he is trying to settle an argument with a friend, say "I'm sorry it is the library's policy not to settle bets and arguments." If the patron says he is working on a cure for cancer, say "I'm sorry it is the library's policy not to assist people working on finding a cure for cancer." Eventually even the stupidest patrons get the message.

HIT THE PATRON OVER THE HEAD WITH AN INSULTING OPENING LINE

Your perky little patron has withstood your offensive body odor, your bad breath, and your rude behavior. Apparently this irksome little twit is not getting the message. It's time now to resort to insults. Here are a few opening lines that you might try: a) You don't look stupid. What is it that you want? b) This better be quick. My legally guaranteed coffee break starts in exactly 15 seconds. c) Not you too. Tell me you don't need help like that last moron who bothered me. d) I'll be glad to help you if you promise not to ask me anything stupid. e) Look I'm having a bad day. I just found out I have a very contagious form of hepatitis. Can't you just leave me alone? f) If you ask me a stupid question I'll start screaming bloody murder.

LAUNCH PERSONAL ATTACKS
WHILE CONDUCTING THE
REFERENCE INTERVIEW

If even after all of that abuse your patron is still hanging in there, you've got one last chance to get rid of him/her. Try a personal attack. Turn the reference question into something very embarrassing. Let's say for example a male patron says that he is doing a research paper on sexual inadequacy in men and needs some information on the subject. Laugh at the patron and say, "Oh just tell the truth. You're impotent and too embarrassed to admit it!" Conducting the reference interview in this manner will get rid of most patrons.

MAKE USE OF ABUSIVE
CLOSURE TECHNIQUES

So things didn't work out this time. You weren't successful in driving your patron away. Don't despair. All is not lost. With the right closure technique you can insure that this nag will never come back. Here are a few suggestions of things to say: a) Now that I've shown you how to find a book in the library you should never need my help again unless you're a complete moron. b) No offense but that was really a stupid little exercise you put me through. c) I didn't get my Master's Degree in Library Science in order to waste my time on such trivia. d) Now that you've taken up five minutes of my time I really expect you to do your own work from now on.

STEER CLEAR OF THE REFERENCE DESK

"Yes your Honor, I'd love
to serve on the O.J. jury."

The best way to avoid reference patrons is to avoid the reference desk. This can be done in several ways: a) Get yourself appointed to the Organizational Review Committee of the American Library Association. You will never have time to do any real work in your library again. That is the main function of A.L.A., to rescue librarians from actually working in a library. b) The next time you get a jury duty summons, offer to serve on the longest trial possible. c) Volunteer for the National Guard and hope that Saddam Hussein starts another war in the Middle East. d) Run over your foot with a loaded book truck and apply for disability leave. e) Spend an inordinate amount of time in the book stacks under the justification that you are working on a very difficult reference question for the Mayor.

Chapter 8

ATTENTION LIBRARY DIRECTORS: HOW TO CARE FOR AND FEED YOUR REFERENCE LIBRARIANS

Every reference librarian knows that there are tons of books on how to care for and feed dogs, cats, parakeets, and even tropical fishes. Why are there no books then on this subject for reference librarians? Lord knows the average reference librarian has a much more difficult life than the average guppy. This chapter is therefore intended to fill that need. Follow the instructions given and we guarantee that the result will be a much happier reference staff. Remember a happy reference staff is a productive reference staff.

Give him a Melvil Dewey cuddle doll.

Shower her with praise.

Provide her with the proper lighting equipment.

Provide her with a nutritious high fiber breakfast.

Take her to Happy Hour once a week.

Let him take home the aluminum cans from the staff waste basket to supplement his income.

Let her do your job for two hours every day.

Give him a V.I.P. parking space for his broken down '79 Chevette.

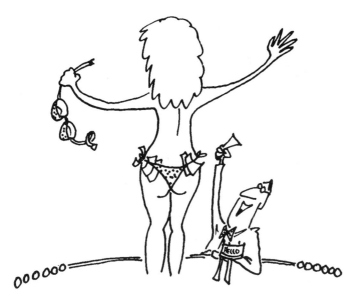

Send him to the A.L.A. conference when it meets in New Orleans so that he will have an opportunity to meet new colleagues and enjoy new experiences.

Feed him chocolate three times a day.

Make every day casual day for them.

Let him be the first to preview the swimsuit edition of *Sports Illustrated* to make sure it is appropriate for the library's collection.

Chapter 9

THE AUTOMATED REFERENCE DESK IN 2001

The library is the only place in today's society where you can experience the full diversity of humankind. The library is a lot like the Statue of Liberty. It welcomes all of our tired and huddled masses. Our doors are always open to the rich and the poor, the well educated and poorly educated, and the young and the old. And let's not forget the good, the bad, and the ugly. The good and the ugly we can handle. We need help, however, fending off the bad. In a recent research project, Professor Elwood E. Elkington of the Eggington Information Studies Institute in Washington, D.C., asked a randomly selected group of reference librarians what technological developments they would like to see by the year 2001. To his surprise, he discovered that reference librarians were for the most part not interested in more sophisticated electronic information delivery systems. Rather they want technological enhancements built into the reference desk to help them deal with abusive patrons. What follows are some of these advancements.

The trap door

The odor activated anti-perspirant pistol

The ceiling mounted electrically activated noose

The 18mm stun machine-gun

The instant lobotomy machine

The voice activated boxing glove

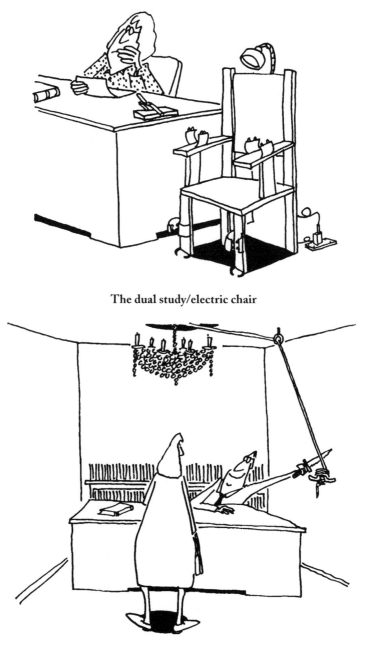

The dual study/electric chair

The movable chandelier

The homicidal ceiling duck activated by the words "I need more."

An automatic tattoo machine that brands people with a tattoo of Bozo the Clown whenever they ask a stupid question.

A brain liposuction machine

A mechanical parrot that screams "Stupid question! Stupid question!" whenever a patron asks a stupid question.

Chapter 10

CONTEMPORARY ISSUES IN REFERENCE LIBRARIANSHIP

While ivory towered professors and trade journal philosophers can wax futuristically about the dawning of our new electronic age, the average reference librarian knows the truth. Yes, things have changed, but they haven't changed all that much. Although more and more material is being released in electronic form, reference librarianship still concentrates on the sometimes satisfying but often maddening process of bringing books and people together.

ISSUE #1: WHAT ARE THE CHARACTERISTICS OF A GOOD REFERENCE BOOK?

The reference collection is the heart of any academic, school, public, or special library. In one compact area of the library it covers everything from aardvarks to zygotes. Reference books come in all sizes and shapes. They range from the eccentric—*The Guinness Book of World Records*—to the bland—*The Standard and Poors Stock Reports*. Some reference books, however, are more useful than others. That's because they have certain important characteristics:

1) There are no weird format features like pop-up illustrations or holograms. Catalogers don't know what to do with weird formats, so they simply refuse to catalog them. As a result they never get on the shelves.

2) They are not arranged in an "easy to steal the page I need" loose leaf binder format (like *The Facts on File Book of Maps*).

3) They are not bound so tightly that when you photocopy them the spine breaks.

4) The copyright date is not printed in Roman numerals to hide the age of the book.

5) They always have Cataloging in Publication data so as to insure quick processing from the Cataloging Department.

6) They are indexed by page not by entry (like the *Encyclopedia of Associations*) to insure that stupid patrons do not continually bring it up to you and say I looked for this term on page so and so but I couldn't find it.

7) They do not give long term weather reports (like *The Farmer's Almanac*) so you won't get sued for rained out picnics.

8) They should be big enough to carry a lot of information, but not so big that you get a hernia pulling them off the shelves.

9) They should be written at a third grade level so as to be understandable to most adult users.

10) They should have glow-in-the-dark spine lettering so that they can be retrieved without a miner's lamp.

11) Their print size should not be so small that the publisher includes a magnifying glass with the book (like *The Oxford English Dictionary*).

12) They should not be divided up into three arbitrary and hard to use parts (like the new *Encyclopaedia Britannica*).

13) They should not be updated solely to make more money for the publisher (like most Gale Research publications).

14) They should be bulky enough to make them difficult to steal.

15) They should be printed on razor proof polyester paper.

ISSUE #2: WHAT DOES THE WELL DRESSED REFERENCE LIBRARIAN LOOK LIKE?

SQUINT
From assisting genealogists with the microfiche reader.

PREMATURE GRAY HAIR
From feigning interest to patrons who simply must tell you their life story while you try to answer 4 ringing phones and other walk-ins.

COKE BOTTLE GLASSES
From too much reading in the O.E.D.

PAISLEY POWER TIE
Thinks it demands respect & makes a great napkin at lunch.

SLOUCHING POSTURE
From getting power tie caught in fax machine.

DISFIGURED DIGIT
From pressing the ESCAPE button on the computer (not sure why but heard that's what you do when all else fails).

SEAT BELT
For buckling up on the information super highway.

WRITING ON HAND
So won't forget e-mail password.

CARPAL TUNNEL SPLINTS
From two finger typing at the public access catalog.

SHIN INJURY
From 1st grader who's dinosaur report was due in the morning and your QE862 shelf was bare.

ROLLER BLADES & PADS
For getting around quickly in the book stacks.

TENNIS SHOES
For running to the photo-copier to add toner, add paper, or unjam it.

Unlike catalogers who like mushrooms seem to be kept in cool, dark back room areas, reference librarians interact with the public. Their outward demeanor and physical appearance, therefore, are critical in influencing how people think about librarians. Therefore it is our strong belief that reference librarians should wear tasteful, modern clothes and sport appealing, contemporary hair styles. But that's not all. They should also be specially equipped to do their jobs effectively, expeditiously, and safely.

ISSUE #3: WHAT DO PATRONS WANT?

Many reference librarians think that this question is an unanswerable conundrum. They think that the mind of the average library patron is an unfathomable mystery. This is not true. What do patrons want? It's actually a simple question to answer. They do not want what they say they want. Why do patrons lie? There are three reasons: 1) embarrassment (Would you rather say "I need books on human biology" or "I need a book on sexual inadequacy in men"?), 2) privacy (Would you rather say "I need a book on crime" or "I need a book on how to kill someone without leaving a trace of evidence"?), or 3) an ulterior motive (Would you rather say, "I need a book on ancient Etruscan art" or "I'd really like to take you out on a date"?).

ISSUE #4: HOW SHOULD REFERENCE SERVICES BE EVALUATED?

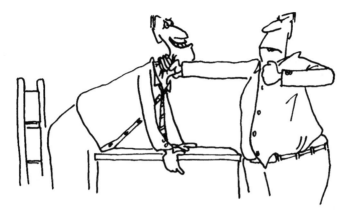

The conventional wisdom is that you should evaluate a library's reference department by the number of questions the staff answers correctly each month. This is an invalid method, however, because the reference librarian is the judge of what is "correct." The patron is the only person who really knows if his or her question was answered correctly. Unfortunately patrons rarely say, "Thank you very much for answering my question comprehensively and correctly." They are never reluctant, however, to voice displeasure, and the more displeasure they voice the more you can be sure that your reference staff is incompetent. That's why the following "Patron Displeasure Index" is a more valid standard to judge your reference librarians by than the traditional "Questions Answered Correctly Index."

Patron Displeasure Index

Phone Calls to the Mayor
Number of Times Flipped Off
Threats of Lawsuits
Actual Lawsuits
Punches Thrown
Punches Landed
Shots Fired
Casualties
Nails in Automobile Tires

ISSUE #5: WHAT ARE THE THREE STAGES OF REFERENCE BURNOUT?

Reference burnout, as we've discussed, is an inevitable part of working the reference desk on a long term basis. Like the big dust ball that grows under your sofa every week, it's something you just can't avoid. There are three stages of reference burnout: 1) first degree burnout which is characterized by eating and sleeping disorders, 2) second degree burnout which can lead to violent acts directed against inanimate objects (photocopiers, computer terminals, and staff lounge vending machines), and 3) third degree burnout which can result in a psychotic episode in which library patrons and other living things may be at risk of physical injury.

ISSUE #6: HOW CAN A LIBRARY DIRECTOR TELL IF HIS OR HER REFERENCE LIBRARIAN IS READY TO EXPERIENCE A PSYCHOTIC EPISODE AT THE REFERENCE DESK?

It is absolutely imperative that an employee who is on the verge of moving into the danger zone of third degree burnout, be gotten off the desk immediately. How can you tell if a reference librarian is at that point? It's a situation that requires constant monitoring. The best way to do this is to hire someone from time to time to pose as a library patron and ask stupid questions. Let's say you send a dopey looking college freshman to the reference desk to ask the question, "What is your best English translation of *Hamlet*?" If your reference librarian answers in any of the following ways, there's a very good chance he or she is suffering from third degree burnout.

1. "Congratulations, that is the stupidest question I have ever gotten in my twenty-five years of being an academic reference librarian, and I've had some pretty stupid students come through those doors."

2. "It's very scary to me that you represent our nation's future."

3. "Do you really think I went to college for four years and graduate library school for two years to waste my time on morons like you?"

4. "By any chance is your name Gump?"

5. "For you I would definitely recommend the Classic Comic Book version of *Hamlet*."

6. "Is there a full moon out tonight or do you always act like an idiot?"

7. "Let me guess, you're here on a football scholarship?"

8. "Someone must have put something funny in the water cooler at the Admissions Office the day they let you in."

9. "Does insanity run through your family?"

10. "Please get out of my sight before I start screaming!"

ISSUE #7: WHAT PRODUCTIVE JOBS CAN BURNED OUT REFERENCE LIBRARIANS DO?

Once you diagnose someone as a burnout victim, what can you do with him or her. Actually there are a number of jobs that these people can do without risking harm to other human beings. Here are some ideas:

1) Flicking the lights on and off fifteen minutes before closing.
2) Watering the plants.
3) Dusting the plastic plants.
4) Stamping out a ten year supply of due date slips.
5) Cleaning out the staff refrigerator.
6) Filing Value Line update pages.
7) Putting trash cans under roof leaks.
8) Making sure that the toilet paper in all the bathrooms rolls from the top down.
9) Watering the library's front lawn with a garden hose.

10) Cutting up old catalog cards to make a ten year supply of scratch paper.

11) Keeping track of all I.R.S. forms.

12) Cleaning out all the pencil sharpeners.

13) Taking down outdated notices and flyers from the bulletin board.

14) Polishing the globe.

15) Keeping a fresh supply of pencils and scratch paper by each computer catalog.

16) Checking each book in the library collection to make sure that its tattletape is still intact.

ISSUE #8: WHAT ARE SOME GOOD SABBATICAL IDEAS FOR BURNED OUT REFERENCE LIBRARIANS?

Extreme third degree burnout victims may not be able to regain their sanity within the library walls. These people may indeed need a rehabilitative sabbatical, but you would be making a big mistake if you sent them on some relaxing and enjoyable project like observing ocean currents off the coast of Maui or studying the ancient Mayan ruins on the beach at Cancun. What long term effect would these idyllic activities have on the reference librarian? True, our burnout victims' blood pressure and pulse rate would certainly decrease but the endemic nature of such an experience would only highlight the chaos and stress of working with problem patrons and stupid reference questions. A return to the reference desk after such a sojourn would be quite problematic. It would in the long run, therefore, be much better to send third degree burnout victims on extremely stressful sabbaticals that would in comparison make life at the reference desk seem sane. Here are some ideas:

1) Volunteer as a United Nations peacekeeper in Bosnia.

2) Study patterns of gang activity in south central Los Angeles.

3) Job share with an air traffic controller at O'Hare Airport during the week between Christmas and New Year's.

4) Become a tribal mediator in Rwanda.

5) Measure radiation levels in Chernobyl.

6) Offer your services as a human crash test dummy at the Ford Proving Grounds in Detroit.

7) Circulate gun control petitions at the local country music bar.

8) Give lectures on the hazards of second hand smoke at the nearest truck stop.

9) Give retirement seminars to convicts with death sentences.

Chapter 11

CRAZY, WACKY, AND STUPID REFERENCE QUESTIONS

At any A.L.A. annual conference it's fun to hang around a cozy group of reference librarians who have hunkered down in the corner of the conference hotel cocktail lounge. Two or three drinks into their little get together and the conversation inevitably turns to reference desk horror stories. You hear about the junior college student who asked for the library's best English translation of *Hamlet* and the village idiot who wants to know where he can buy a can of checkered paint. From conversations like this, from my own personal experience, from the trusted words of reference librarians I have known over the years, and from my *American Libraries* survey on reference librarians, I have compiled what I consider to be the definitive list of off beat reference stories. The one thread running through all these stories is that they are all true!

• A freshman in college during the first day of classes at a large eastern university asked for "the recipe you use to make toast." In response the reference librarian said, "You mean French toast?" and the student replied, "No, I need the recipe for regular American toast."

• A high school student preparing a report on the White House called up his public library and wanted to know "the shape of the Oval Office and the type of flowers grown in the Rose Garden."

• A man called up a county library reference department and wanted to know if the library was a government "suppository."

• Sometime in the late 40's or early 50's when such matters were articulated more delicately than they are today, a young man of 18 walked up to the reference desk at the Detroit Public Library and asked if the library had information on positions. The reference librarian said, "You'll find the occupations materials in that alcove on the other side of the card catalog." The patron replied, "Oh, I didn't mean that. What I wanted was when people get married they have positions."

• A few weeks after the installation of a new computer catalog a confused patron came up to the reference desk and said, "The computer says to press any key but I can't find the any key. Can you show me where it is?"

• A third grade public school student inquired of her school librarian if she had an audio recording of live dinosaurs. Even worse was the junior high biology teacher who called to find out what color the skin of the tyrannosaurus rex was!

• A middle school student asked his school librarian if she had any books in Spanish. The librarian handed the student a list of Spanish titles held by the library. "How do you know these books are in Spanish?" was the student's reply.

• A graduate student walked into his university's science library and said that he needed to know the method of creating latex from the goldenrod plant. After the librarian found him the answer he told her that he hoped to capitalize on the safe sex movement by manufacturing his own condoms. "What do you think would be a good name for my condoms?" he asked the librarian. Without missing a beat she replied, "Goldenrod Condoms."

• A foreign student studying at a Canadian university was apparently having a struggle with the English language so he approached the reference librarian and asked, "Do you have a writer's clitoris?" Taken aback, the librarian thought hard and answered, "No but I do have a writer's thesaurus." After handing the student the book she added, "I do have a clitoris, but I'm not a writer!"

• The librarian at a western historical society library once got a call from an enthusiastic young hiker who wanted to know "the exact locations of all of the lost mines and buried treasures in the Rocky Mountains." This same librarian also got a call from a local television news broadcaster. He wanted a photograph of St. John the Baptist.

• In a very busy public library with a line of six people at the reference desk a patron insisted on knowing "Why are the largest islands found in oceans?" Several weeks later at the same library a patron called up on Thursday March 24 and asked, "Is today Good Friday?"

• A high school senior walked up to his school librarian and asked for information on "youth in Africa." The librarian responded, "Oh, you want books about growing up in Africa?" The student shook his head and said, "No, I want books about killing old people and vegetables." After a nanosecond of confusion, the librarian replied with a straight face, "Oh, you don't want books on youth in Africa; you want books on youth in Asia."

• The reference department of a large eastern university was divided into four subject divisions. Sometimes this caused confusion. For instance, one day a man called up the Science Reference Desk and asked, "Do you have venereal disease in your division?" The librarian quickly replied, "Yes, but you have to come to the library to get it."

• A woman once called a public library branch reference desk and asked for a recording of hiccups. The librarian on duty assured her that such a recording was not available in her branch but suggested that she try the central library's music department for sound effects recordings. The woman replied that she had no way to get to the central library to pick the recording up. She then asked if the reference librarian couldn't hiccup several times over the telephone while she tape recorded it at the other end!

• A sophomore in college approached the reference desk and asked "Was Leonardo da Vinci a Christian or a homosexual?"

• An undergraduate student majoring in business administration walked up to the reference desk of a midwestern academic library and asked for help in selecting a topic on which to write an assigned research paper. The topic had to be about some business aspect of a foreign country. At the time NAFTA was very much in the news so the reference librarian suggested that the student consider the issue of free trade between Canada and the United States. The student looked the reference librarian in the eye and said with a tone of indignation that the topic had to deal with a foreign country. When the librarian attempted to assure the student that Canada is in fact a foreign country, the student went over to an adjacent index table to enlist support from two other students. Luckily, neither student was a

Canadian, but both knew better than she that Canada is indeed a sovereign nation.

• Another illustrious undergraduate scholar who obviously did not major in geography or international relations asked his reference librarian the following question: "Is the correct term Swedish or Swiss?" The startled reference librarian quickly came to his wits and responded, "Yes!"

• A man approached a reference desk of a medium sized eastern community and asked for a list of activities being offered in Jerusalem during Holy Week. He planned to take 10,000 Christians on a pilgrimage to the Holy Land where they would all gather on the Mount of Olives at sunrise on Easter morning.

• A man called the reference desk of a southern public library and wanted to know the blue book value of a Chevy half-ton pickup truck. "What model?" asked the reference librarian. He didn't know. "What size engine?" He didn't know. "Long bed or short bed?" He didn't know. "Well," said the librarian in exasperation, "what can you tell me about the truck?" "Oh," said the caller, "it has a gun rack, a hound dog, and a sticker of the Confederate flag on the back window."

• A young man asked his reference librarian what kind of wood you should use to drive into the heart of a vampire.

• Many of us have had patrons (especially undergraduates taking an introductory philosophy course) approach us and ask us for the answer to the meaning of life. But have you ever had a patron ask "Who invented music?" That was a question that an academic reference librarian received a couple of years ago in a large eastern university library. How did she respond? "I have absolutely no idea!" was her answer.

• That was not, however, the most difficult reference question which that librarian has ever been called upon to answer. Ordinarily that most frequently asked question of all time—"Where is the bathroom?"—is not a very difficult query to answer. In this librarian's library, however, the men's room and the women's room were in two different directions. This is an important detail because the gender of the patron asking the question was not easily recognizable. What did the librarian do? She briefly considered conducting a reference interview to determine the person's sex (Do you prefer sitting or standing?) and then decided that her question to the earlier question of who invented music was even more appropriate in this instance. "I have absolutely no idea where the bathrooms in this building are!" she said and then quickly headed up to the staff lounge for her mid-morning coffee break!

• An elementary school librarian reports that at Christmastime students are often given an assignment to research the Christmas customs of foreign lands. One little third grader asked her for help in finding this information for the country of Mauritania. Not only did the library have no information on Christmas customs in Mauritania, it also had no information on Mauritania. So what did the librarian tell the student to write? She said, "At Christmastime in Mauritania you hope to get invited to an embassy party!"

• An undergraduate taking an introductory course in human sexuality approached his reference librarian and wanted to know what a "trisexual" was.

• A junior high school student requested that his school librarian find him a picture of the locomotives that ran on the underground railroad.

• A junior college student told his reference librarian that he needed a photograph of Jesus Christ. "You mean a photograph of a statue or painting, don't you?" responded the librarian. "No," the student responded with firmness, "I need an actual photograph."

• Perhaps that junior college should strengthen its history curriculum because another student there wanted a videotape of Abraham Lincoln giving the Gettysburg Address. When he was informed that this was not available he responded, "Gee, you really ought to think about getting it. You have videotapes of Clinton, and Lincoln was a much greater president than Clinton."

• A public library reference librarian reports that she was once asked the question, "What is the proper procedure to follow in giving your deceased dog a funeral?"

• An academic reference librarian reports that one evening a man called to ask, "What was the name of the little boy in Holland who put his finger in the dike?" The librarian actually found one source that said that the boy's name was Hans. When this was reported to the patron he responded, "It is not!" and slammed down the phone.

• Another student in a large southern university proclaimed to his reference librarian, "Y'all don't have a copy of *Jane Eyre!*" In reply the librarian said, "Oh, that can't be. *Jane Eyre* is a classic. I'm sure we must have it. What did you look under?" The student responded, "I looked in the card catalog under Eyre, Jane."

• A very frustrated public library patron expressed disappointment to her reference librarian that she could not find a book that was published in

1965. "Where did you try to find it?" asked the confused librarian. "In the catalog drawer numbered 1965," the patron replied.

• A high school student asked his school librarian for "a book on mountain airiest." The librarian's first impression was that the student needed a book on mountain areas. After a lengthy reference interview, the librarian decided that the kid needed a book on Mount Ararat. It turned out, however, that she was still wrong. After further questioning, she finally decided that the student was interested in Mount Everest, but to this day no one knows for sure!

• A woman in her mid forties walked into a large southwestern public library and said she was looking for a book about Martin King. As the reference librarian repeated her request, the patron added helpfully that she thought that Martin King's middle name was Luther. "Oh," responded the librarian, "perhaps you are looking for a book about Martin Luther King. "That's probably right," replied the patron, "after all it is for my son." Dutifully the librarian went to the stacks and pulled out a book entitled *The Life of Martin Luther King, Jr.* "Oh no," said the patron, I don't want that one. I want a book about the famous King, you know the father."

• In a medical library, a certified physician approached the reference librarian and said, "I know that the medical journals are arranged alphabetically by title but where is the journal entitled *Lancet*?" "Try looking under the "L's," responded the librarian.

• Amateur genealogists are often in the middle of weird reference situations. Take, for example, the patron who approached her public library reference librarian and said, "I'd like you to download my great-great-grandfather's Civil War pension file from the Internet. After all, it's all on computer somewhere." The librarian responded by saying, "Oh, I wonder if the National Archives is aware of this new development."

• Another genie junkie approached the same librarian and said, "My great-great-grandmother was born in 1876, but I don't know her parents' names or where they lived. So I'd like to look at the 1870 census." The librarian responded by saying, "Am I missing something here?"

• A women called up the reference department of a large midwestern public library and asked for a book that would help with her husband's "impudence." I don't quite understand the problem," responded the librarian. "Is your husband a sharp tongued and mean spirited person?" "Oh, no!" responded the patron, "my husband is a wonderfully kind person. He just can't seem to get it up any more."

• In the late 1970s a Congressman from the state of Louisiana was arrested in a Washington, D.C., bathroom for performing an act of sodomy. This scandal made the front page of newspapers all over the country, and piqued the curiosity of millions of taxpayers. One woman in a medium sized midwestern city read the newspaper and called the library. "I want to know what the word "sodomy" means," she asked.

The reference librarian was startled by such an X-rated request so early in the morning by such an elderly woman. "You want what?" he stammered incoherently into the phone.

"I just read the morning paper," responded the woman, "and I saw an article about a Congressman from Louisiana performing an act of sodomy in a public bathroom." The reference librarian now had his bearings and told the woman to hang on while he grabbed the dictionary. At this very moment it just so happened that the President of the Library Board and the Chair of the City Council were hanging around the reference desk. This was the morning that they were to be given an "in the trenches" look at the important questions that reference librarians answer every day. Budget negotiations between the Library Board and City Council were to begin tomorrow morning.

Not wanting to offend either official, the reference librarian picked the least offensive definition he could find in *Webster's Unabridged*. "According to the dictionary," said the librarian in his softest telephone voice, "sodomy is an unnatural sex act."

"I know that!" screamed the woman into the telephone. "I want to know what that unnatural act consists of!"

Keeping a wary eye on the Mayor and Board President who now seemed to be very interested in the "important" kinds of questions fielded by the reference department every day, the librarian dove back into his *Webster's Unabridged*. There were no shortage of definitions. Sodomy appeared to be a large umbrella term for a diverse array of interpersonal forms of physical communication. After several minutes of consideration, the librarian settled on one definition and returned to the phone. "According to Webster," he said, "sodomy is an unnatural sex act between an animal and a human being."

"Hmm," said the patron dumbfounded, "I wonder what kind of animal was in the bathroom with that Congressman."

• A woman walked up to the reference counter in a large western public library and asked for a biography of a woman named "Rosetta Stone."

• Another patron at that library put up a very big fuss because he did not think that a book of ancient Greek myths should be shelved in the nonfiction area. He said that "he did not want to put things into his brain thinking they were real when they were not."

• Yet another patron came in and declared, "Several years ago I read a book that was published in the 1970's. Can you tell me where the books from the 70's are shelved?"

• "What is the punishment for crime in Russia?" was the query of a patron who wandered into a large east coast city library.

• A ninth grade teacher (teacher!) walked up to her school librarian and asked for biographical information on Miss Jane Pittman (a fictional character)!

• A middle aged man (obviously suffering from a mid-life crisis) matter of factly walked up to his public library reference librarian and said, "I have to go to New York City next week on business and I'd like to know the name of the street where all the hookers hang out."

• A high school science student asked his school librarian for a book that would describe the effect of pollution on orgasms. "You mean organisms," said the librarian quickly. "Yes," said the now red faced student, "I meant organisms."

• An elderly woman explained to her reference librarian that she had sent her deceased pet poodle to a company in Florida to have it freeze dried. The company never sent the poodle back. The woman wanted to know where she should send her complaint.

• A concerned parent wanted to know if her infected child could give his chicken pox to his pet hamster.

• A teenager wanted Elvis Presley's Internet address.

• A college student (college!) wanted to know if the *New York Daily News* came out every day.

• A woman called the reference desk of a public library and asked for the phone number of the body parts store in Pittsburgh. The librarian pulled out the yellow pages and asked, "Is it a foreign or domestic car?" The patron replied, "Oh no, I need the number for the body parts stores, you know where they get kidneys and livers and such." The librarian determined that she wanted the phone number for the Organ Donor Bank.

• A freshman arrived at the reference desk of his academic library and in great confusion said, "This library is much different from the one I used in high school. Is there any order at all to the way the books are shelved?"

• A parent called up her public library and said, "My child is required to come up with five great explorers and all I have been able to think of are Einstein, Edison, and Franklin. Can you give me two more?"

• A student in a Canadian university called her reference desk and asked what the academic requirements were to get into graduate library school. When told that she must have at least a strong B average, the student replied, "That's too high for the salaries that librarians make!"

• A patron in a midwestern public library created a big stir when he went up to the reference desk and demanded $230. "Why do you think we should give you that money?" asked the reference librarian. "You owe it to me as damages," he replied. "What damages?" asked the librarian. "The damages I incurred for using your *Farmer's Almanac*." Now the librarian was totally bewildered. "Please explain," she said to the patron. "Well, last year I came in and used your *Farmer's Almanac* to plan my company picnic. I picked out a week that the almanac said would be fair and sunny. It rained and I had to rent the Elks Club for $230!"

• In an Idaho public library a patron called the reference desk and declared that he had information that during the previous year United Nations troops had fired on and killed civilians in the state. The patron proceeded to relate a good deal of detailed information about the incident, including the approximate date, the name of the small town, and the number of black helicopters involved. Then he asked the reference librarian to find proof that the incident had occurred. The librarian then looked through a multitude of magazine and newspaper indexes and came up empty. When she called the patron back to tell him that she could find no documentation of the incident, the patron replied, "Well, of course you can't find any information. They completely covered it up!"

• In a Texas library a man from Southern California wandered in and said, "Can you direct me to a metaphysician. I looked in the yellow pages and couldn't find any metaphysicians listed." The patron proceeded to tell the reference librarian that he had walked to Texas from California. He conducted his journey by walking in the direction the light was green at each intersection he encountered.

• Reference librarians typically get directional questions as well as informational ones. We've all had our share of where's the bathroom type questions but how many have had a patron ask (as one did in a large midwestern public library), "Is that the elevator that goes up and down?"

• In an eastern public library a reference caller identified herself as an "elderly woman in her 90's." She wanted to know the nearest state in which she could be married without a blood test and a waiting period. When the reference librarian explained that she would have to travel some distance to do this, the patron replied, "Oh, the Hell with it; we'll just shack up together."

• An amateur genealogist walked into a southeastern public library and asked "What year was the 1790 census done?"

• Don't you just love parents who try to do their children's homework assignments? Sometimes they're much better off leaving it to the kids. Consider the dedicated father who came into his public library and asked for information about "some guy in radio whose name was spelled Mark Coney." After spending quite a bit of time futilely looking for information about Mr. Coney, the reference librarian was relieved to learn from the man's third grade son that the radio guy's name was really spelled "Marconi."

• The legal arena is an area that many reference librarians have to be knowledgeable about in order to meet the needs of their patrons, but sometimes this is very difficult as in the case of the frantic man who rushed up to the reference desk of his public library and demanded to see a copy of the "riot act." The very startled reference librarian responded "What?" and the patron exclaimed, "My boss wants me to read the riot act to a bill collector who has been bothering him and I need a copy of it!"

• A high school student working on a history project wanted some information on a "dude named Malcolm the Tenth."

• Another high school student wanted to see a book with lots of autographs so that he could pick one to model his signature after.

• How's this for a good excuse to look at *Playboy Magazine*? A college professor requested the "Women of the Ivy League" issue because he'd heard a book of his was a prop in the centerfold picture.

• An old man went to his library to find out what he could do about getting a poltergeist out of his '83 Chrysler New Yorker.

• Another man quietly expressed his desire to have the phone number for the Mafia.

• An earnest junior high school student wanted information on the famous rocket scientist, "Warren Van Buren."

• Another student wanted to see a newspaper from the day Jesus was born. He said a microfilm copy would be all right.

• A young man who was looking for the *Reader's Guide*, asked for "The Periodic Table of Magazines."

• A young woman who was doing a research paper on President Kennedy requested that her reference librarian help her find information on Ozzy Osbourne. "Why do you want information on him?" asked the librarian. "Don't you know," responded the student, "that he is the man who shot Kennedy?"

• A high school student who asked for a book on mammograms really needed the book *Culturegrams*.

• A beginning genealogist requested "the book with all the dead people listed in it."

• The mother of a college student told her reference librarian that her daughter needed to do a paper on an English wolf who wrote poetry a long time ago. It turned out that she needed information on the book *Beowolf*.

• Another patron asked for the book *The Spy Who Couldn't Get Warm*. It turned out she needed *The Spy Who Came In from the Cold*.

• A man who was having trouble finding a particular phone number went up to his reference librarian with the phone book in his hands and asked her, "What part of the phone book carries the unlisted numbers?"

• "What are the causes of snakebite?" asked a high school student.

• A pet lover asked her reference librarian for a book of sign language for deaf dogs.

• A college student wanted to know the name of the man who invented the time machine!

• And finally a high school student asked his reference librarian to explain the difference between gynecology and genealogy!

Chapter 12

A SURVEY
OF REFERENCE
LIBRARIANS

The purpose of this book has been to attempt to describe the life of the average reference librarian. A great deal of research went into this project. I talked to literally hundreds of reference librarians, observed them at work, interviewed hundreds of their patrons, and even spent a great deal of my own time working the reference desk. All of that was helpful, but I still needed to reach out and connect with thousands of other reference professionals to get the complete picture. That's why I ran a survey in my "Will's World" column in *American Libraries*. What follows are the results from that survey.

WHAT GIVES REFERENCE LIBRARIANS THEIR GREATEST ON THE JOB SATISFACTION?

1) A heartfelt thank you from a patron, 2) A fair and livable salary, 3) Sincere appreciation from administration, 4) An occasional evening and weekend off, 5) Chocolate, 6) Having a patron say, "When do you work next? I'd like to have you again," 7) Having a student or co-worker say, "You know everything. Where can I find...," 8) Teaching a patron how to use a source and then seeing that patron return to use the source by himself, 9) Finding the right answer after a long search, 10) Knowing the exact location of an item, no matter how obscure, off the top of my head.

WHAT ONE RESOURCE DO REFERENCE LIBRARIANS VALUE THE MOST?

1) The local newspaper; 2) The local telephone directory; 3) Their memories; 4) The library's catalog; 5) *The World Almanac*; 6) *Webster's Unabridged Dictionary*; 7) *NADA Used Car Price Guide*; 8) INFOTRAC; 9) In house files of past reference questions; 10) Other reference librarians.

WHAT BAD HABITS DO
REFERENCE LIBRARIANS HAVE?

1) Spending all my free time surfing the Internet rather than reading books, 2) Coming to work early, 3) Leaving work late, 4) Letting myself be obsessed with unanswered reference questions, 5) Distrusting all library administrators, 6) Rolling my eyes at stupid questions, 7) Suddenly developing P.M.S.-like symptoms upon seeing certain patrons, 8) Eating a chocolate candy bar as a reward for answering a rough reference question, 9) Grumbling under my breath at stupid patrons, 10) Finding a place to hide in the stacks to flatulate, 11) Finishing the sentences of stupid patrons, 12) Packrat tendencies—holding on to anything that I think might help me

answer a reference question, 13) Getting too personal with reference interviews especially if the patron is very handsome, 14) Interrupting the patron during the reference interview, 15) Yawning when boring patrons ask boring questions, 16) Running red lights, 17) Being arrogant and impatient with patrons, 18) Drinking too much coffee and then going out to the reference desk with a caffeine buzz, 19) Insulting street people who panhandle in the library parking lot, 20) Laughing at patrons behind their backs, 21) Refusing to bend library policies even for people who have had cancer operations, 22) Holding a grudge against patrons I don't like, 23) Keeping people on hold for ten minutes or longer, 24) Asking catalogers in the break room how the back log is going, 25) Stealing candy out of co-workers' desks, 26) Doing token work on tough reference questions just before I'm due to get off the desk, 27) Screaming aloud in pain whenever anyone mentions the name, "Rush Limbaugh," 28) Treating personal friends and relatives like reference patrons, 29) Engaging in compulsive helping behavior, 30) Preferring to do it myself rather than teaching patrons how to do it, 31) Telling patrons what they don't want to hear, 32) Purposefully staying ignorant of the ways of genealogy.

WHAT KIND OF PATRONS BUG REFERENCE LIBRARIANS?

Patrons 1) who believe that reference librarians exist to help them use the photocopy machine, 2) who order you to do something because they are "paying" your salary, 3) who are too lazy to come to the library to do their own simple but time consuming research, 4) who believe that reference librarians have nothing to do but sit around and wait for their questions, 5) who approach you in restaurants to ask a reference question, 6) who think you are as interested in their family tree as they are, 7) who ask you to appraise their antiques over the telephone, 8) who watch you demonstrate the use of the OPAC for fifteen minutes and then say "Could you do that again after I get a pencil and paper to write it all down?", 9) who call the reference desk and ask you to do their children's homework, 10) who

feel compelled to tell you their life story as a preface to their reference question, 11) who ask for help and then try to tell you how to look something up, 12) who call on the phone and ask for all the information you have on a broad subject like water pollution or Native Americans, 13) who make you go through hoops to locate an item and then decide that they don't want it after all, 14) who send you on wild goose chase for book and periodical titles that do not exist, 15) who ask unanswerable questions like how many wild birds starve each year in the state of Maryland, 16) who cannot understand why we do not have books written solely about their family tree, 17) who refuse to do their own work even after you have spent 20 minutes showing them how to use a source, 18) who ask you if you had to go to college to "do this," 19) who put their hands on you and call you sweetie, baby, or honey, 20) who ask you "Do you work here?" when you are standing behind the reference counter and are wearing a badge clearly marked STAFF, 21) who come up to the desk and ask to borrow not only a piece of paper and pen but also some white-out, an envelope, some scissors, and a ruler, 22) who insist on asking a reference question while you're on the phone answering another reference question, 23) who complain to the director that you weren't helpful when you spent over a half hour working on their idiotic, unanswerable reference questions, 24) who are in the county jail and who call up with very complex legal questions, 25) who ask questions while sucking on pens, pencils, toothpicks, or straws, 26) who call from bars and expect you to drop everything to settle a bet on some incredibly lame subject like who had the most R.B.I.'s in the National League in 1939, 27) who come to the library with P.M.S., 28) who look sinister and ask for books on devil worship, 29) who expect customized service on obscure subjects and expect it *now*, 30) who think we just sit around all day and read books 31) who believe that *Consumer Reports* evaluates everything they want to purchase every year, 32) who expect you to make long distance calls for free for them in pursuit of an answer to a question, 33) who waste my time by fumbling through a briefcase, backpack or oversized purse to find a crumpled piece of paper with the note they made to themselves and then can't read their own writing, 34) who beg to check out reference books "just for overnight," 35) who persuade you to allow them to check out a reference book "just for overnight" and then never return it.

WHAT KIND OF CATALOGERS BUG REFERENCE LIBRARIANS?

Catalogers 1) who eat all the ice cream at the annual library staff picnic, 2) who refuse to change idiotic Library of Congress subject headings, 3) who refuse to change idiotic Library of Congress classification numbers, 4) who refuse to ask for input from the reference staff, 5) who refuse to work even one hour a week at the reference desk to find out what the real world is like, 6) who take the bestsellers home with them as soon as they arrive from acquisitions, 7) who refuse to give higher priority to books in demand by the patrons, 8) who procrastinate cataloging non-book materials, 9) who dress like slobs and then complain about their image, 10) who talk in MARC in front of non-catalogers.

WHAT KIND OF TEACHERS AND PROFESSORS BUG REFERENCE LIBRARIANS?

Teachers and professors 1) who check out entire subject areas and never bring the books back on time, 2) who expect fine and fee waivers, check-out extensions, and multiple renewals simply because they are "educators," 3) who assign research papers without checking with the library to determine that it has the resources to enable the students to complete the assignment, 4) who treat reference librarians like their own personal clerical support, 5) who give assignments that their students do not understand, 6) who expect you to put a rush order on any book they want, 7) who do not think that librarians should make as much money as they do, 8) who make no effort at all to do their own reference work, 9) who abandon their students in the library with no warning at all and then retreat to the faculty lounge for a coffee break, 10) who think that librarians are lower down the human scale of evolution, 11) who require everyone in their class to read a particular title even if the library only has one copy of it, 12) who forget to put required reading titles on reserve, 12) who tell their students to complain to the librarians that they should expand their collections in a particular area, 13) who send their problem students down to the library to keep them from disrupting the class, 14) who think knowledge of the alphabet or decimal system is beneath them and expect me to find everything for them.

WHAT KIND OF FANTASIES DO
REFERENCE LIBRARIANS HAVE?

1) That the President of the United States will call me with a reference question; 2) That Robert Redford will call me with a reference question; 3) That Robert Redford will make a movie about a reference librarian and will ask me to move in with him to help him write the script; 4) That Robert Redford will come into my library, fall in love with me, and say, "Let me take you away from all this madness"; 5) That a high school student will come in and ask for help on gathering at least 30 minutes before closing; 6) That a high school student will some day say thank you 7) That any patron will say thank you; 8) That my director will take the time to work the reference desk at least two hours a week to get a taste of the real world; 9) That I will be paid enough to support a family of one; 10) That I will be able to come up with a logical answer to the question, "Why do you keep doing reference work?" 11) That I will find the time to formulate a decent fantasy; 12) That I would have an unlimited budget for

on-line searching; 13) That I would be able to act like a heavy metal guitarist while showing thousands of adoring, scantily clad female patrons how to use *Granger's Index to Poetry*; 14) That I could find an actual photograph of Jesus Christ; 15) That patrons could learn to ask questions without telling their family history beforehand; 16) That my library could afford to buy all the reference sources it needs; 17) To be able to insult patrons for asking stupid questions without being fired; 18) That I would have enough "off desk" time to complete worthwhile projects; 19) That I could answer a reference question for the Library of Congress; 20) That I had the nerve to make anonymous calls to teachers to tell them which parents do their children's homework assignments; 21) That patrons would put the newspapers back in order, return books to the shelves, and push in their chairs after they leave; 22) That I would be given carte blanche access to the Facts on File warehouse and told that I can have anything and everything that my heart desires.

WHAT EPITAPHS WOULD REFERENCE LIBRARIANS LIKE TO HAVE ON THEIR GRAVESTONES OR ASH URNS?

1) Contact me through Necronet; 2) Can I call you back? 3) The Bathroom is to the right; 4) Go find it yourself; 5) Quiet! 6) Dying is easy; reference is hard; 7) Kiss my gravestone; 8) I'm sorry I can't help you anymore; 9) You want what? 10) I may not have had all the answers but I knew where to find them; 11) Here lies reference man; 12) Bother someone else for a change; 13) Closed for business; 14) Take your questions to someone else who is stupid enough to work nights and weekends for peanuts; 15) Logged off; 16) All your stupid questions drove me to an early grave; 17) She didn't look like a librarian; 18) Could you hold please?

Index